OUR EARTH IN ACTION

MOUNTAINS

Chris Oxlade

FRANKLIN WATTS

LONDON•SYDNEY

First published in 2009 by Franklin Watts

Copyright © 2009 Franklin Watts

Franklin Watts
338 Euston Road
London NW1 3BH

Franklin Watts Australia
Level 17/207 Kent Street
Sydney, NSW 2000

A CIP catalogue record for this book is available
from the British Library.

Dewey number: 551.43' 2

ISBN 978 0 7496 9024 3

Printed in China

Franklin Watts is a division of Hachette Children's Books,
an Hachette UK company. www.hachette.co.uk

Artwork: John Alston
Editor: Sarah Ridley
Design: Thomas Keenes
Editor in Chief: John C. Miles
Art director: Jonathan Hair
Picture research: Diana Morris

Picture credits:
Bryan & Cherry Alexander/Alamy: 21. Mikhail Basov/Shutterstock: front cover, 1.
Bruce Block/istockphoto: 27. Rob Brock/istockphoto: 11. Bryan Busovicki/Shutterstock: 12t.
EVRON/Shutterstock: 30b. Justin Horrocks/istockphoto: 29t. Dave Logan/istockphoto: 19.
Jennifer London/istockphoto: 4-5b. NASA: 5t, 12b, 14. Andrew Penner/istockphoto: 17.
Piskunov/istockphoto: 16b. Igor Plotnikov/istockphoto: 25. Rest/istockphoto: 18.
Ashok Rodrigues/istockphoto: 13. Pupo Celso Rodrigues/istockphoto: 16t.
Noah Srycker/Shutterstock: 22. Stone/Getty Images: 20. Visuals Unlimited/Getty Images: 9.
Ingmar Wesemann/istockphoto: 23. Gary Yim/Shutterstock: 28. *Every attempt has been made
to clear copyright. Should there be any inadvertent omission please apply to the publisher for
rectification.*

CONTENTS

ABOUT MOUNTAINS

Mountains are places on the Earth's surface where rocks rise high above the surrounding landscape. They are built up by colossal forces that squash, stretch and fold the Earth's crust. The world of the high mountains is very different from the world on the plains below.

THE MOUNTAINOUS EARTH

Mountains cover about a quarter of the Earth's surface. Some mountains are 'free-standing', which means they are single mountains in a flat landscape. But most mountains are part of mountain ranges. The world's great ranges, such as the Himalayas and the Andes, stretch for thousands of kilometres and contain hundreds of towering, snow-covered peaks.

CHANGING THE LANDSCAPE

Mountain ranges are built up over hundreds of millions of years. They are pushed thousands of metres upwards as rocks are slowly folded or lifted on a huge scale. Mountains are also built up by eruptions of molten rock from underground.
Just as the forces of nature build mountains, they

▼ A typical mountain scene – snow-capped rocky peaks rising above the plains.

knock them down again. The rocks of mountains are slowly worn away by the actions of wind, flowing water, and especially ice. This cycle of building and wearing away has been going on for billions of years, and there are remnants of vast mountain ranges all over the Earth. Most of the mountain ranges we see today have formed in the last 250 million years.

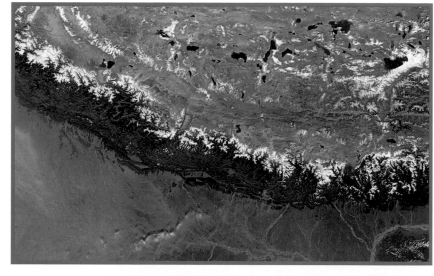

▲ A satellite image of part of the Himalayan mountain range. The white areas are snow.

IN THE MOUNTAINS

The environment on mountains is different from the environment around them, perhaps only a few kilometres away. The climate is colder, wetter and more windy than below on the plains, and on the peaks the ground is rocky and icy, so no plants can survive. These conditions make it challenging for people to live in the mountains. Mountains also affect the weather around them, making some places wetter and others drier.

When is a hill a mountain?

There is no official height at which a hill becomes a mountain. Whether a hill is called a mountain depends on the local landscape and traditional names. A hill 2,000 m high might be thought of as a tall mountain in one area of the world, but merely a foothill in another.

EARTH'S STRUCTURE

Mountains are built up by the slow, gradual movements of the rocks that make up the Earth, and by new rocks being formed. To see how these processes work we have to understand the structure of the Earth and what is going on deep under the surface.

THE CRACKED CRUST

The Earth has four main layers — the inner core, the outer core, the mantle and the crust, which is the outer layer. The Earth's crust is up to 70 km thick under mountain ranges and as little as 6 km thick under the oceans. The crust and top layer of the mantle form a layer called the lithosphere. It is cracked into many giant pieces called tectonic plates. These move around slowly, at just a few centimetres a year.

▼ *The internal structure of the Earth, showing the layers.*

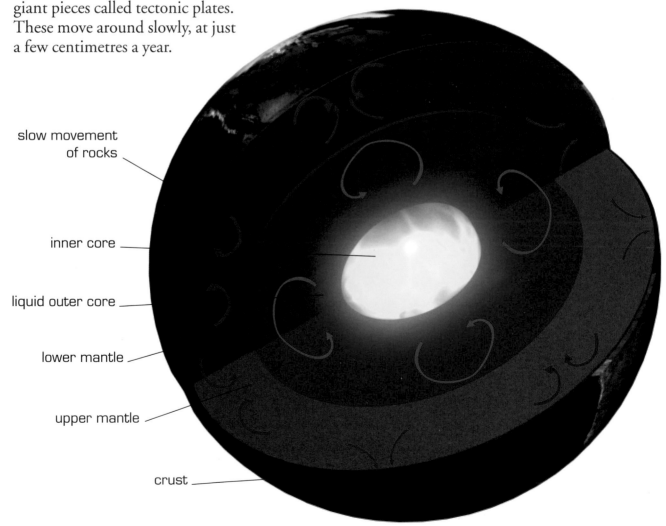

slow movement of rocks

inner core

liquid outer core

lower mantle

upper mantle

crust

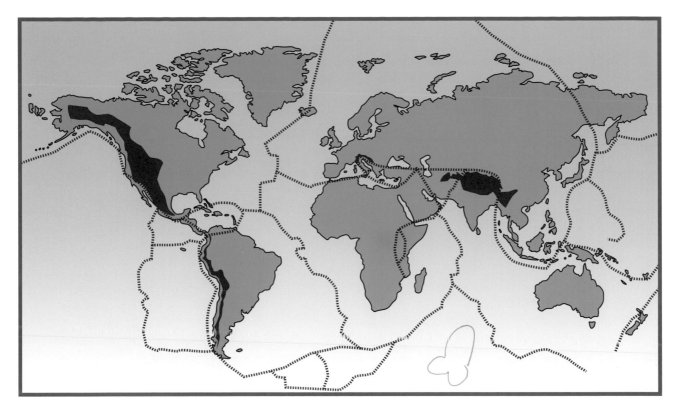

PLATE BOUNDARIES

A plate boundary is a line where one plate meets another plate. There are three types of boundaries — conservative, constructive and destructive. At a conservative boundary, the two plates slide past each other in opposite directions. At a constructive boundary the two plates move apart. At a destructive boundary, the two plates move towards each other. Here the plates can be two thin ocean plates, two thick continental plates, or one of each.

▲ The Earth's major mountain ranges (red areas) lie along boundaries between tectonic plates (red lines).

WHERE MOUNTAINS FORM

The location of mountain ranges is closely linked to tectonic plate boundaries. Most mountains form at destructive plate boundaries. Here, the collision between the plates crumples the edges of the plates, pushing up mountains. Volcanic mountains form along destructive and constructive plate boundaries. Where a volcano remains active, the mountain can be pushed up relatively quickly by the magma that forms deep beneath the Earth's crust. Finally, the movement of the tectonic plates can break up the Earth's crust, to form huge blocks of rock that thrust up to become mountain ranges.

Types of rock

All mountains are made up of three types of rock. Igneous rocks are made where magma (molten rock) cools and solidifies. This can happen underground or on the surface at volcanoes. Sedimentary rocks are made from layers of sediment (small particles of rock) that are deposited on sea-beds or river-beds. Metamorphic rocks are made when other rocks are changed by immense heat and pressure, often deep under mountains.

FOLD MOUNTAINS

There are three main types of mountain, named after the way they are formed. They are fold mountains, block mountains and volcanic mountains. Here we look at fold mountains. You can find out about block mountains on pages 10-11 and volcanic mountains on pages 12-13.

FORMATION OF FOLDS

All the major mountain ranges on Earth, such as the Alps and the Himalayas, are fold mountains. Fold mountains form where layers of rock are squashed by the movement of tectonic plates. This happens at destructive boundaries. As the plates move towards each other, the rocks at their edges crumple up, forcing them to fold. The tops of the folds are forced upwards, building mountains. Because tectonic plates move very slowly, it takes millions of years for a mountain range to be formed.

SUBDUCTION AND COLLISION

Where one of the plates at a destructive boundary is an ocean plate, this plate slides under the much thicker continental plate. It moves down into the mantle below and eventually melts. This process is called subduction. Sedimentary rocks from the ocean plate and rocks from the continental plate crumple to form fold mountains.

Mountains and earthquakes

Earthquakes occur frequently in mountain ranges formed at destructive plate boundaries, such as the Himalayas. They happen because the plates' edges are cracked by the huge forces; the cracks are called faults. As the plates move, the rocks each side of the faults tend to move in jerks rather than smoothly, causing earthquakes.

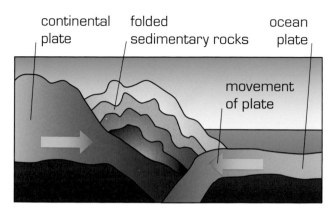

▲ Fold mountains being formed at a destructive boundary between continental and ocean plates.

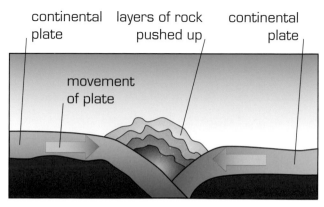

▲ Fold mountains being formed at a destructive boundary between two continental plates.

Where both plates are thick continental plates, there is no subduction. Instead, the plates collide head on, pushing rock both up and down. The mountains grow upwards, and rock pushes downwards, forming huge roots that support the mountains. The crust can be twice its normal thickness where plates collide like this.

▲ Layers of rock folded by immense forces. Folding like this on a giant scale creates mountains.

EVIDENCE OF FOLDING

There is plenty of evidence that rocks are folded to form mountains. Sedimentary rocks are formed in flat, horizontal layers, but in many places we find sloping layers and even vertical ones. Sometimes we see layers of rock in giant folds in cliff faces, bending up and down. Each fold can be many kilometres across or just a few metres across.

BLOCK MOUNTAINS

A block mountain is a mountain that is a giant block of rock. Block mountains are formed where blocks of rock rise or fall because the crust is stretched or squashed by the huge forces generated by the movement of tectonic plates. The Harz Mountains in Germany and the Sierra Nevada in North America are good examples of block mountains.

FAULTS AND MOVEMENTS

A fault is a weak area or crack in the rocks of the Earth's crust. Forces from the movement of tectonic plates create faults and make the rocks on each side of existing faults move. There are several different types of fault. For example, a normal fault is where the rocks on each side of a fault move up and down because the rocks are stretched apart. And a reverse fault is where the rocks along a fault move up and down because the rocks are squashed together. In most cases, faults are complex, with rocks moving up and down, from side to side and twisting as well. A fault may only move once every hundred years, and the size of each movement is normally only centimetres or metres. But over millions of years the total movement can add up to hundreds of metres.

RIFTS AND HORSTS

Block mountains normally form where a block of rock with a fault on each side falls or rises. A rift valley forms where stretching causes a block to fall, leaving higher blocks on each side. These higher blocks form mountains on each side of the valley. A horst block forms where rocks fall on each side of another block. This leaves a mountain standing above the ground on either side.

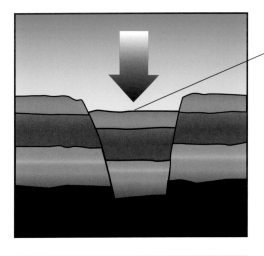

rift valley

◀ *Formation of a rift valley, with mountain ranges on each side.*

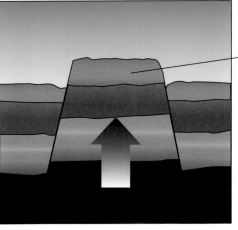

horst block mountain

◀ *Formation of a horst block mountain, where a block of rock rises or where blocks of rock on each side drop.*

The Great Rift Valley

The Great Rift Valley in Africa stretches nearly 5,000 km from Mozambique to the Red Sea. This rift valley has formed over the past 50 million years where the crust is being stretched, and is still growing. There are mountains up to around 5,000 m high on each side. There are also volcanoes, such as Mount Nyiragongo and Mount Kilimanjaro, where magma has leaked through the broken crust.

▼ *Mountains of Africa's Great Rift Valley.*

VOLCANIC MOUNTAINS

▲ *An explosive eruption at a destructive boundary, in this case in Hawaii.*

A volcano is a place where magma (molten rock) from deep under the crust comes to the Earth's surface. Volcanic eruptions build mountains from the lava and ash that is erupted. Volcanoes can be part of mountain ranges, or single, isolated peaks.

VOLCANOES AT PLATE BOUNDARIES

The majority of volcanoes form at the boundaries between the Earth's tectonic plates. At constructive boundaries, magma rises where plates are moving away from each other. The magma forms lava on the surface, which builds up in layers to form mountains. The volcanoes of Iceland and the Great Rift Valley have grown over constructive boundaries. At

Hot spots

A hot spot is a place where magma from the mantle pushes its way up through the crust far from any plate boundary. The magma is thought to come from huge pockets of magma called mantle plumes. The most famous hot-spot volcanoes are those on the Hawaiian Islands. These have grown over a hot spot under the Pacific tectonic plate. Over millions of years a whole chain of mountains has formed as the plate has moved slowly over the hot spot. The islands are actually the tips of enormous mountains that have grown up from the sea-bed (see page 15 for more about undersea mountains).

▶ *An aerial photo of some of the volcanic Hawaiian Islands.*

destructive boundaries, magma is formed where an ocean plate sinks into the mantle and partly melts. The magma forces its way upwards through the crust and creates volcanoes. These volcanoes are often part of ranges of fold mountains along the plate boundary.

VOLCANO SHAPES

Volcanoes come in various shapes and sizes, but most are either composite cone volcanoes or shield volcanoes. A composite cone volcano (or stratovolcano) is a steep-sided, cone-shaped mountain, made up of layers of ash and lava. Composite cone volcanoes form at destructive plate boundaries. They are made of loose material and are often unstable, and their tops can be blown off during violent eruptions. Shield volcanoes have gently sloping sides. They are built up from layers of lava that flow down their slopes. They are called shield volcanoes because they are shaped like an upturned warrior's shield.

▼ *Lava flowing into the sea and solidifying, slowly building up a new volcanic mountain.*

MOUNTAIN RANGES

Most mountains are part of large collections of mountains called mountain ranges, mountain chains or mountain belts. Some ranges contain just a few peaks, but others contain thousands. Large ranges are often divided into sub ranges and groups. The Himalayas is a mountain range that is still growing; other ranges are ancient and are being eroded away.

BUILDING MOUNTAIN RANGES

A map of the world's major mountain ranges and tectonic plates (see page 7) shows that most mountain ranges follow the line of plate boundaries. Large mountain ranges are normally long and thin in shape. This is because they form along the boundaries. The same folding movements or block movements happen right along a boundary, so that mountains are built right along it, too.

▲ *The Caucasus mountain range (top-right) in eastern Europe, seen from space.*

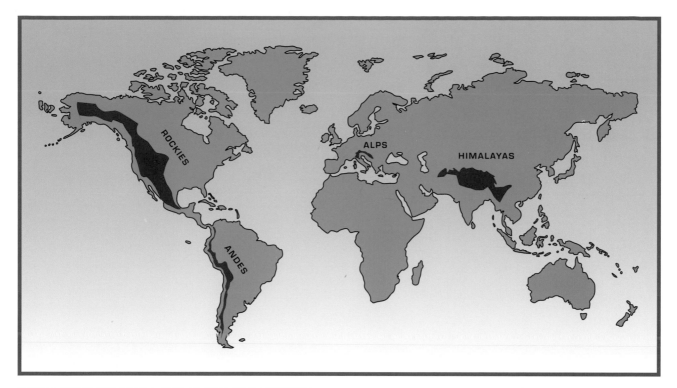

▲ *The world's major mountain ranges.*

THE WORLD'S GREAT RANGES

Here are some of the world's major ranges and how they were formed.

- **Himalayas, Asia** Formed by a collision between the Eurasian and the Indian tectonic plates. The world's highest mountain range.
- **Andes, South America** Formed along a destructive boundary between the Nazca and South American plates. The world's longest mountain chain.
- **Rockies, North America** Formed at a destructive boundary between the Pacific and the North American plates.
- **Alps, Europe** Formed by a collision between the African and Eurasian plates.

MOUNTAIN RANGES AS BARRIERS

The world's mountain ranges form physical barriers between the parts of the world on either side. In the distant past, they prevented people from migrating to populate new areas of the world. The Himalayas can still only be crossed in just a few places. They have kept Mongolian and Chinese people to the north separate from Indian people to the south, so the two groups of people have very different languages and customs.

Ranges under the sea

Many volcanic mountains are under the sea. Long mountain ranges form at constructive boundaries. The Mid-Atlantic Ridge under the Atlantic Ocean can be thought of as the world's longest mountain range. At some destructive boundaries and hot spots, volcanoes called seamounts grow from the sea floor. Mauna Kea in Hawaii rises 10,203 m from the sea floor, so some call it the world's tallest mountain.

WEARING DOWN MOUNTAINS

As mountains are slowly built up, so they are slowly worn away again. In the distant past, vast mountain ranges have been formed and then worn down into today's gentle hills.

Some of today's mountain ranges are remnants of once higher mountain ranges that have stopped growing and are now being destroyed by weathering and erosion.

WEATHERING

Weathering is the breaking down of rocks into small pieces, and is the first stage in the wearing away of mountains. Ice weathering is the most destructive type of weathering on mountain tops. It happens when water trickles into cracks in rocks and then freezes. The water expands slightly when it freezes, and this opens up the cracks. If the ice melts and then freezes again, the cracks enlarge.

▲ Sugar Loaf Mountain in Rio De Janeiro, Brazil, is the core of a volcanic mountain that has been eroded away.

▼ A jumble of rocks shattered by weathering cover this mountain slope.

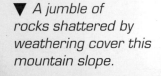

Eroding folded rocks

The rocks in fold mountains are weak because they have been folded and broken as the mountains were formed. This allows them to be weathered and eroded more quickly than if they were made of solid rock, and is why mountain peaks are often made up of shattered heaps of loose rock.

Other types of weathering in mountains include onion-skin weathering, where surface rock expands and contracts because of alternating hot and cold temperatures, chemical weathering, where rainwater slowly dissolves rocks, and biological weathering, where plant roots split up rock. Weathered rock is easily eroded.

▲ *The turbulent water of mountain rivers carries rocky particles down from the mountains and onto the plains below.*

EROSION

Erosion is the wearing away of rocks by wind, flowing water and ice. High winds may move loose particles, allowing them to roll down slopes. Flowing water carries material with it into streams and rivers. Fast-flowing river water pulls loose rocks from the river-bed and banks, and particles in the water knock out more loose rock. Gradually streams and rivers erode gulleys and steep-sided valleys in mountain slopes. The rivers carry the rocky material away to the plains below. Erosion by water is greatest when snows are melting and rivers are flooding. Glaciers also erode mountains (see pages 18-19). On mountains, loose material on cliffs and steep slopes is also carried downhill by gravity.

GLACIERS

Glaciers are slow-moving rivers of ice. They form over thousands of years from layers of snow that fall in high mountains. Over many years the weight of snow at the top squeezes the snow below into a thick sheet of solid ice. Gravity forces the ice to creep down the mountainside.

GLACIER FLOW

Glaciers flow downhill in valleys, as rivers of water do. They continue flowing until they reach a level where the air temperature is warm enough to make the ice melt. This lower end of a glacier is called its snout. Glaciers can be hundreds of metres deep and more than a kilometre across. They flow at any speed from 1 or 2 cm per day to 2 or 3 m per day. As glaciers turn corners or flow onto steeper ground, cracks called crevasses appear in them.

▲ *Underneath this glacier, ice is gouging away at the rocks, eroding a valley.*

GLACIAL EROSION

Glaciers erode away the rocks they flow over. The ice itself pulls the rock apart as it flows over them, but most erosion is caused by rocks dragged along the ground by the ice. In high mountains, glaciers are responsible for more erosion than wind and water together. Rocky material is carried along under the glacier, inside it and on top of it. When the ice melts at the glacier's snout, the material is dumped on the ground, forming mounds of rubble. This is then washed away in streams that carry water away from the melting glacier.

GLACIAL LANDFORMS

Over thousands of years, glaciers erode U-shaped valleys in the landscape. We can see these valleys if the glaciers melt away. There are many U-shaped valleys in the northern hemisphere that were formed thousands of years ago during the last ice age. Then much of the northern hemisphere was covered with a thick layer of ice. Other glacial features include cirque (or corries), which are armchair-shaped dips in mountain slopes, arêtes and sharp peaks.

▼ *A typical glacial valley. The glacier that created it has long since melted away.*

MOUNTAIN WEATHER

Typical mountain weather is wet, cold and windy. It makes high mountains dangerous places to be. Even on a day when it is warm and sunny in the valleys around a mountain, it can be freezing cold with gale-force winds on the mountain tops thousands of metres above.

DROPPING TEMPERATURES

The temperature in the atmosphere falls by about 1°C for every 100 m you move up. That means if the air temperature is a warm 20°C on the valley floor it will be 0°C on the mountain 2,000 m higher up. On the summits of the world's highest mountains, the temperature never rises above freezing. Most rain starts life as snow, which melts as it falls through warm air. In mountains the snow lands before it reaches the warmer air below, so snow regularly falls in mountains. There is always a visible snow line on high mountains, above which snow always falls instead of rain.

▼ Freezing temperatures and high winds are a serious threat to mountaineers.

MOUNTAIN WINDS

Wind is squeezed as it rises to flow over mountains, which means its speed increases. Winds also increase in strength as they blow through gaps between mountains. The summits of the world's highest mountains can be buffeted by high-level winds called jet streams, which can blow at hundreds of kilometres per hour.

CLOUD AND RAIN FORMATION

Mountains create their own weather because of the way air moves over them. Clouds form when humid air (air that contains water vapour) rises. As it rises, it cools, and the water vapour turns to droplets of liquid water, which make up clouds. When winds carrying humid air hit mountains, the air rises up the mountain slopes, which makes clouds form. This is why there are often clouds over mountains when the rest of the sky is clear, and is also why mountains get plenty of rain.

▲ *These clouds have formed as humid air is forced up and over the mountains.*

Rain shadows

Because humid air forms clouds and rain as it rises over mountains, it loses much of its water vapour. When the air descends down the other side of mountains, it is quite dry, and so the land here gets very little rain. This effect from the mountains is known as a rain shadow.

MOUNTAIN CLIMATES AND ZONES

Climate is the pattern of weather a place experiences over a long period of time. There are different climates at different places on a mountain. For example, the base of a mountain may have warm summers and cool winters, but its summit may experience cool summers and very cold winters. Different plants and animals live in these climates.

CHANGING CLIMATES

The climate is generally cooler, wetter and windier on mountains than on the plains and in the valleys below. This does not mean it is cold, wet and windy every day, but on average, the temperature is lower, rainfall (or snowfall) is higher, and winds are stronger. Winters are also longer, and summers shorter. On the summits of the highest mountains the climate is similar to polar climates experienced in the Arctic and Antarctic. Even in summer, temperatures are sub zero, and storm-force winds and snow storms are common.

▼ In tropical regions, forests grow on the cloudy, wet mountain slopes.

PLANTS AND ANIMALS

Mountain slopes can be divided into three different climate zones, called, from bottom to top, montane, sub-alpine and alpine. The position of the zones depends on the plants that live there. The plants that live in one zone cannot survive in the harsher conditions in the zone above, and so there is a line where vegetation changes that shows the boundary between one zone and the next. These are the typical plants found in each zone:

- **Montane zone** Conifer forests (pines, firs and spruces), with trees shaped so that snow falls off them. They have needles instead of leaves, so they can survive being frozen.
- **Sub-alpine zone** No forests, but stunted conifers because of high winds, or low shrubs that are not damaged by winds.
- **Alpine zone** No trees. Small flowering plants that survive on little water, and cope with the cold. Above a certain altitude, nothing can survive.

▲ *In the alpine zone, flowering plants come to life during the short spring and summer.*

Thin mountain air

As you move up through the atmosphere, the air becomes thinner and thinner, and so there is less oxygen for animals to breathe. Animals that live high in the mountains (in the sub-alpine and alpine zones) are adapted to survive with less oxygen. See also page 28.

CASE STUDY: THE HIMALAYAS

The Himalayas form the world's tallest mountain range. It contains nine of the top ten world's tallest mountains, including Everest, the tallest, at 8,850 m. The range stretches nearly 2,500 km from northeast India to Pakistan, and is up to 400 km wide from north to south. The word Himalayas means 'abode of the snow' in the Sanskrit language.

▲ *Location map of the Himalayas.*

HIMALAYAN WEATHER

The Himalayas lie between the north Indian plains to the south and the Tibetan Plateau to the north. There is a huge range of climates, from sub tropical (warm with heavy seasonal rains) in the southern foothills to polar in the high peaks, where there is permanent snow and ice. The Himalayas have a huge effect on climates around them. They trap warm, humid southerly winds blowing up from the south, causing heavy monsoon rains. Their rain shadow lies to the north, and keeps the Tibetan Plateau very dry. They also keep northern India warm by stopping Arctic winds from the north. The Himalayas are drained by several major rivers, including the Indus, the Ganges, the Brahmaputra and the Yangtze.

▶ *A view across the Himalayan foothills to the spectacular lofty peaks.*

FORMATION OF THE HIMALAYAS

The Himalayas were formed by the collision between the Indian and Eurasian tectonic plates. These are both continental plates, and their rocks have been pushed up into fold mountains. The collision started about 70 million years ago, where there was originally a sea, and the mountains began to rise about 50 million years ago. This makes the Himalayas among the youngest mountains on Earth. The Indian plate is still moving northwards, so the Himalayas are still growing, but only by a few centimetres per year. Earthquakes set off by the movement of the plates are common in the Himalayas.

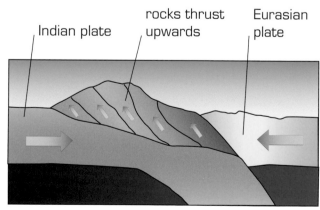

Indian plate   rocks thrust upwards   Eurasian plate

▲ *The Himalayas were built up as two tectonic plates collided, piling rocks on top of one another.*

Himalayan people

Very few people live in the high valleys,
where the winters are long and cold.
However, the southern foothills are densely
populated. Deforestation is a problem here,
and causes frequent landslides. Travel is
slow, despite some modern roads, and
there are only a handful of mountain passes
through the range.

CASE STUDY: THE ANDES

The Andes is the world's longest mountain range. It runs 8,000 km along the west coast of South America, starting near the Caribbean Sea and finishing in the south of Chile. The Andes contains the highest mountains outside Asia, along with several active volcanoes.

▲ Location map of the Andes.

ANDEAN FEATURES

The Andes is generally about 300 km wide. At the northern end it divides into three distinct chains, parallel to each other. In the central area it is wider and there are two plateaus that lie between mountains to the west and east. These are called the Andean plateaus. Lake Titicaca, 190 km long, is on one of these plateaus. The highest mountain in the Andes is Aconcagua, in Argentina, at 6,962 m high. There are more than 200 active volcanoes.

ANDEAN CLIMATES

Because the Andes stretches from the tropics nearly to Antarctica, it experiences a wide range of climates. At the northern end there are tropical forests on the mountain slopes, and the peaks are free of snow for some of the year. At the southern end there is permanent snow at low levels and glaciers flowing down from the summits. Humid winds blowing from the east dump their rain when they hit the Andes. Much of it flows back to the sea through the Amazon river basin. The Atacama Desert lies in Chile in the rain shadow of the Andes. It is the driest place on Earth.

FORMATION

The Andes mountains began forming between about 140 and about 65 million years ago and are still growing. They lie over a destructive boundary between the South American and Nazca plates. They are a combination of fold mountains and volcanic mountains formed by subduction of the Nazca plate.

▶ Spectacular rock towers in Patagonia, at the southern end of the Andes. Erosion has worn away softer rock, leaving the hard core exposed.

Life on the plateau

The Andean plateaus, at between 3,600 m and 4,000 m above sea level, are some of the highest inhabited places on Earth. People grow crops and raise animals such as the llama. Lake Titicaca is the world's highest navigable lake. It has towns and villages on its shores and islands. Close by is La Paz, the largest city in Bolivia, and the highest major city in the world.

LIFE IN THE MOUNTAINS

Even though the world's mountains are sparsely populated compared to the plains, millions of people choose to live in them. Most make their lives here because generations of their families have done so, and often because they are part of ethnic groups that have lived here for hundreds of years. They have learned how to survive mountain life.

MOUNTAIN FARMING

Most mountain people survive by farming in high mountain valleys. Only some crops can grow in mountain areas because of the harsh climate. Animals adapted to the climate, such as sheep, goats, llama, and yak, are raised for meat, fur, milk and transport. They are normally moved to lower ground during winter.

▲ Farmers build terraces on the mountain slopes to increase land area and trap water.

MOUNTAIN RESOURCES

We make use of mountains for more than just farming. Tourism is a major industry in many of the world's mountainous regions. People travel to the mountains to enjoy the scenery, to walk and climb on the mountains, and to ski on their slopes. Mountain areas are also a good source of hydroelectric power, as the climate is often wet and rivers flow through steep-sided valleys suitable for dams.

DRAWBACKS AND DANGERS

Life in the mountains brings many problems. Mountain towns and villages are normally remote, and mountain roads are twisty, and often

closed during winter because of snow or landslides. After heavy snow fall, avalanches threaten places at the foot of mountain slopes. Altitude sickness (or mountain sickness) is another problem for people visiting the mountains. This is caused by the lack of oxygen in the thin mountain air, and causes sickness and headaches. People who are raised at high altitude in the mountains are adapted to cope with low levels of oxygen. Volcanoes bring their own dangers of lava flows, ash avalanches (called pyroclastic flows) and mud flows, but people live around them because they offer excellent soil for growing crops.

MOUNTAINS IN THE FUTURE

The mountains that people live in and play on today are only temporary features on the Earth's surface. In tens of millions of years even the vast mountain range of the Himalayas will have been eroded away. But the world's tectonic plates will keep moving for billions of years to come. So entirely new mountain ranges, perhaps even higher than the Himalayas, will take their place.

▼ Dams in the mountains provide water and hydroelectricity for people in towns and cities on the plains below.

GLOSSARY

ash tiny particles of solidified magma

block mountain a mountain formed where huge blocks of rock rise or fall

climate the long-term pattern of weather that a place experiences

conservative plate boundary a line along which the edges of two tectonic plates slide past each other

constructive plate boundary a line along which two tectonic plates are moving apart

continental plate part of a tectonic plate under a continent, which is much thicker than an ocean plate

crust the rocky top layer of the Earth

deforestation the cutting down of forests for fuel and to create space for farming

destructive plate boundary a line along which the edges of two tectonic plates are moving towards each other

erosion the wearing away of the landscape

eruption the emission of lava, ash or gas from a volcano

fault a crack in the rocks of the Earth's crust

fold mountain a mountain formed when rocks are squeezed together and folded up

foothill a hill or mountain between the plains and the tallest mountains of a mountain range

glacier a slow-moving river of ice

global warming the gradual warming of the Earth's atmosphere

gravity the force that attracts all objects to the Earth

hot spot a place far from any tectonic plate boundary where magma forces its way to the surface

hydroelectricity electricity generated by water power

ice age a period of time in the past when the climate was colder than today and thick ice sheets covered much of the northern hemisphere

lava the name given to the molten, rocky part of magma when it comes out of a volcano

magma molten rock underground

mantle the thick layer of rock inside the Earth under the crust

mountain a place where the Earth's surface rises high above the surrounding landscape

mud flow a fast-flowing mixture of volcanic ash and water

northern hemisphere the part of the Earth's surface that lies north of the equator

ocean plate part of a tectonic plate under the ocean, which is much thinner than a continental plate

plain a broad flat area of land

plate boundary the line along which two tectonic plates meet

plateau an area of flat land in a mountain range

range a collection of mountains

seamount a volcano that grows up from the ocean floor

sedimentary rock rock formed when layers of sediment are laid down on top of each other over millions of years

tectonic plate one of the huge pieces that the Earth's crust is cracked into

volcanic to do with volcanoes

volcano a place where magma emerges onto the Earth's surface from under the crust

weathering the breaking up of rocks into smaller particles

Further information

EVEREST
Lots of information on Everest from the US Public
Broadcasting Service.
http://www.pbs.org/wgbh/nova/everest/

GLOBAL VOLCANISM PROGRAM
Information on active volcanoes around the world.
http://www.volcano.si.edu/

GOOGLE EARTH
Downloadable software that displays the world in 3D — great for
exploring the world's mountain ranges.
http://earth.google.com

HYDROELECTRICITY
Explanation and animation on hydroelectricity.
http://www.youtube.com/watch?v=htT_8sFJx1w

MOUNTAIN WEBSITE
School website all about mountains.
http://www.woodlands-
junior.kent.sch.uk/Homework/mountains.htm

NASA
A catalogue of visible Earth images from NASA. This page includes
images of many mountain ranges, including some in 3D.
http://visibleearth.nasa.gov/view_set.php?categoryID=810

NATIONAL SNOW AND ICE DATA CENTER
US organisation site pages all about glaciers.
http://nsidc.org/glaciers

NOTE TO PARENTS AND TEACHERS:
Every effort has been made by the Publishers to ensure that the
websites in this book are suitable for children, that they are of the
highest educational value, and that they contain no inappropriate or
offensive material. However, because of the nature of the Internet, it
is impossible to guarantee that the contents of these sites will not be
altered. We strongly advise that Internet access is supervised by a
responsible adult.

INDEX

Here are the lists of contents for each title in **Our Earth in Action**:

Volcanoes
About volcanoes • Earth's structure • Where volcanoes happen
Composite cone volcanoes • Shield volcanoes and cinder cones • Lava • Volcanic ash
Volcano hazards • Living with volcanoes • Volcano science
Case study: Mount St Helens • Case study: Pinatubo • Giant eruptions

Earthquakes
About earthquakes • Plate tectonics • Where earthquakes happen
Earthquake waves • Effects on the landscape • Tsunamis • Effects on buildings
Living with earthquakes • Building for earthquakes • Earthquake science
Case study: Kobe 1995 • Case study: Kashmir 2005
Case study: San Francisco

Rivers
About rivers • Rivers and landscapes • Upper river stages • Middle river stages
Lower river stages • River science • Floods • Flood protection • River resources
Dams • Case study: The Mississippi • Case study: The Nile • River problems

Weather
About the weather • Earth's atmosphere • Air pressure and winds
Clouds and rain • Weather fronts and systems • Tropical storms • Extreme weather
Seasons • Recording the weather • Weather forecasting • Climates
Adapting to climates • Climate change

Mountains
About mountains • Earth's structure • Fold mountains • Block mountains
Volcanic mountains • Mountain ranges • Wearing down mountains • Glaciers
Mountain weather • Mountain climates and zones • Case study: The Himalayas
Case study: The Andes • Life in the mountains

Seas and Coasts
About seas and coasts • In the oceans • The seabed • Mountains and trenches
Tides and currents • Waves • Coastal erosion • Coastal features
Beaches • Estuaries and deltas • Sea and coast resources
Case study: The Pacific • Environmental issues